This Notebook Belongs To

____

Made in United States
North Haven, CT
14 June 2023

37726414R00067